# Travelling Music

Books published by the author:

## POETRY

*Music from Home: Selected Poems*
*Winters Without Snow*
*Lie and Say You Love Me*
*Queen of the Ebony Isles*
*Bone Flames*
*What Madness Brought Me Here: New and Selected Poems*
*Travelling Music*

## SHORT FICTION

*Jesus and Fat Tuesday*
*Driving Under the Cardboard Pines*

## NONFICTION

*Speech and Language Development of the Preschool Child*
*A Long Way from St. Louie: Travel Memoirs*
*Over the Lip of the World: Among the Storytellers of Madagascar*

## CHAPBOOKS

*The Mules Done Long Since Gone*
*Looking for a Country Under Its Original Name*
*Talkstory*

# Travelling Music

Colleen J. McElroy

*Story Line Press*
*1998*

Published by Story Line Press, Inc.
Three Oaks Farm
PO Box 1108
Ashland OR 97520–0052

This publication was made possible thanks in part to the generous support of the Nicholas Roerich Museum, the Andrew W. Mellon Foundation, and our individual contributors.

Grateful acknowledgment is made to the following for permission to reprint previously published material:

Anna Akhmatova, from *The Complete Poems of Anna Akhmatova*, translated by Judith Hemschemeyer, edited by Robert Reeder. Copyright © 1992 by Judith Hemschemeyer. Reprinted by permission of Zephyr Press.

Theodore Roethke, "The Waking" in *The Collected Poems of Theodore Roethke* by Theodore Roethke. Copyright © 1992 by Theodore Roethke. Reprinted by permission of Bantam Doubleday Dell Publishing Group, Inc.

Ntozake Shange, from *For Colored Girls Who Have Considered Suicide When the Rainbow is Enuf* by Ntozake Shange. Copyright © 1975, 1976, 1977 by Ntozake Shange. Reprinted by permission of Scribners, a division of Simon & Schuster.

Elva Perez-Tervino, "Character Sketch of a Woman Looking" in *Cuentos: Stories by Latinas*, edited by Gomez, Moraga, and Romo–Carmona. Kitchen Table Press, NY 1983.

Lynn Haney, from *Naked at the Feast: A Biography of Josephine Baker*. Dodd Mead, NY 1981.

*Painting by Kabuya Pamela Bowens, Transition Triptych, 1990*
*Book design by Paul Joseph Pope*

Library of Congress Cataloging–in–Publication Data

McElroy, Colleen J.
    Travelling music / Colleen J. McElroy
       p. cm
      ISBN 1-885266-65-0
    I. Title.
    PS3563.A2925T73  1998
    811'.54—dc21                                98-36751
                                                CIP

# Acknowledgements

The following poems have appeared originally in: *Kenyon Review*, "Heavy in the S-Curves," "A Little Travelling Music," "Trompe L'oeil: Slovenia," "Lifting the Morning"; *River Styx*, "Five Black Beauties Romancing Dalmatia," "Way Out Wardell Plays Belgrade"; *Massachusetts Review*, "Drawing in the Dark"; *Manhattan Review*, "A Skardalija Walk in Three-Quarter Time," "What the Jackrabbits Know," "Delsey in the Window," "Light Reflecting Glass in the Evelyn Room"; *Seattle Review*, "There's an Obi in the Dishwasher"; *Dramatist Guild Quarterly*, "Sojourn at the O'Neill Summer Theatre: 1987"; *Images*, "A Charleston for Florence Mills"; *Ploughshares*, "Sprung Sonnet for Dorothy Dandridge," "Bo Jangles Visits the Studio," "Paris Subway Tango," "Caution: This Woman Breaks for Memories"; *Brilliant Corners*, "Fascinating Rhythm," "Eads Bridge Boogie Across the Mississippi."

# Contents

**III**

# Part One

*No foreign sky protected me . . .*
*survivor of that time, that place*

*—Anna Akhmatova*

# Under Skies with No Views

*book: a written document; an oath; a bet; arrest;*
*an account; [dial] a quick ticket out; escape*

Fighting what the pillow holds at night
familiar as the corners of your mouth
you are once again stuck in a book

Poor insomniac, trying to escape into
what happens next while the moon
rains its patient light upon the page

Just take it as it comes—never lying
still—otherwise morning will find you
trapped inside tales thick as German busses

chapters articulated for conceit of movement
At least aboard a bus you could hope
for comfortable seats and air filtered for impurities

albeit filled with hissing tourists
taking their latest voyeuristic
swing through someone else's living room—

each offering their version of the best
churches, classic monuments or ruins
and more than they have ever seen beyond

guard rails of allusions   Careful or you will travel
landscapes where the sky is tangerine bright
with promise and the ground rolls out plush as carpet

over plots twisted in symbols and personal bottlenecks
Remember: all memory is dicey at the border and despite
some writer's claim of well-measured beginnings and endings

not every turn of events is artsy or quaint
Watch while we all grope for a new twist to old lines
—tickets punched for the latest disaster as if

no one has ever told us shit happens all over and all
our revelations of the universe come in the dead of night
before we've unpacked that new lover

placed like a vase on the mantle above the bed
Finally if none of this can keep you awake:
the politics that never quite works

the middle–class money and good intentions
the stamp of old metaphors grounded in bestsellers—
one more bad rewrite of someone else's history and

narratives like fat–ass tourists with too many cameras—
just watch the sky grow paper–thin with light
and let yourself wander off the page into sweet

sleep where you dream beautiful oceans
and water that desires nothing for itself

# A Little Travelling Music


*A little travelling music, professor, if you please.*
                                    —a vaudeville exit cue


This is not a planet I would want to inherit—
With its inventory of mountainous sorrows
There is hardly a place to lay a good night's
Sleep before tomorrow's bad news arrives,

And hardly a road I want to travel.
I know these woods are no longer gentle
And love no longer runs through dry grass
Clean as the country we once dreamed of—

Out here hard times grind into thin skin
With needle tracks and pock marks
That make the going rough even for those
Of us who have gone straight.

Listen to the reports: arteries and arterials
Twist and back up all the way out, cyclists
Spin out in heavy water and trashy sunlight.
Long distance hauls jackknife in lanes too narrow

To carry weight limits for any major move, and I can't
Get home—can't get back to ghettos where uncles drove
Jitneys because white cabbies couldn't read the English
Of broken street signs, even in broad daylight.

I want something more than a two-lane either-or
World still mapped by tribal law, or my grandmother's
Reflection stuck black in a window, watching the traffic
Of each year move faster, sighing: "Chile, we all gotta go

When the wagon comes." And when it comes—its door open wide
And curtains blowing, I want more than the temptation to see if
I've arrived at century's end without stumbling over bad memory.

# Atmospheric Pressure

*Anti-war demonstrations:*
*Seattle, Washington and*
*Brooklyn, New York*
*—January 1990*

in the beginning they are no more
than village stragglers silhouetted in dim
light  ragged lines come for a Bastille
showdown in two cities at the nation's bookends
they will cross more or less the same bridge
move at a steady clip   one   two abreast
three here  there five six   brave and scared
heavy air swallows their chants in
sudden bursts   percussion of footsteps
immediately my memory fills in the rest

it is 1966 and automatically
I look for the dogs
cattle prods   firehoses   men
on horseback with holsters that pull
in brutal light  now all light is   a roadster
sleek   American made  it jockeys into place
along the line  accelerates  fast forward
back   forward  moves its  single muscular  rage
irrational as an unruly tape unraveled
off a bent reel   a hinge let go
from the ugly rust of an old screw

the line swarms   regroups   screams
fists  curses  squander the light
the air   a shroud wet and cold
half–blind I could not fail to read   this
horror  distress  released in shrill voices
how could he   and who   and where did he go
and the car  red  did you read the license
no  she's down   blood–chilled in sudden silence
stars shatter  weep  what peace can we
ask of horizons where  violence rides
the tattered fabric of the sky  and the face
of the land dies inside  its own disaster

# The Verdict: Los Angeles 1992

the cities are burning
under the snick–snick of snipers
the metallic stench of overpriced
stores and polyester politicians
sidewalks curl back in flames
this fire has burned since slave
rebellions
ask the old folks who recall the fever
while young black men fight the choke
of authority again and again
their collars a necklace of blood
the rest of us are locked in the syntax
of justice

and I awaken once more in this dream

of my country's greatest shame
the television screen emits a foul odor
its grey–suited terror pulsing failure
a promise
hanging in the air like loose skin
or what burns in neighborhoods where brutality
is the virus and oppression the plague—
a fury feeding
fury that does not begin on the streets
but with fear spread at suburban
tables like rancid butter separating
Them from Us

on the hour every hour rage

seeps in like acid rain
headlines bloom and the media cashes in
commentators ignite flames of old riots
the Judas trees of city halls bear fruit
the stray bullet looks to get the job done
and from police Choppers voices boom:
*(Go To Your Houses! We don't want another hot
summer! How can you destroy your own homes?)*—
but what there is to own when sky
is the only roof and the landlord picks

his way through rubble demanding rent
even as the ashes cool
and iron roses grow in vacant lots

—the cities are burning

on a freefall where my nightmares of yesterday
are no longer a breath away
walls of graffiti sprout a new crop of Tags
the death toll rises
old folks weep as daughters turn
to stone and sons shout
*Enough! Enough!*—
and still the firebird comes shaking
its awful wig of destruction
bearing down on storefronts and churches
on houses carpeted in old slogans
on outmoded generals and demented senators
until we all claim more kinship
with the dead than the living

in the wake the cities die

fires lick my living room
frame by frame
the walls explode
floors creak with each footfall
while the moon rises inside blazing
buildings and spills its children
on a mattress of ashes
a nightmare
explosion where the invisible
grab the hunger of power and prance
in the afterglow becoming momentarily
visible

# The Sight to See

another country and faces that carry
reflections of cousins speaking
languages I've only imagined
another set of women with hips
legs  eyes like my mother's mother
skin polished by the same old sun

another harbor  another airport
and flight attendants with ready
trays of mystery food
another customs clerk
capricious as the weather
one more day cut by mountain ridges
glowing in various shades of purple

another line of bright-eyed children
and easy giggles   their grown-up
counterparts pocketing tips and maps
to lost places   promises of another
day of clocks turning backwards
and ladies wearing too much history

trapped in the tradition of mirrors
where like mama says: folks think
they looking cute but looking curious
another mirror surprised as I am
to find me here ignoring passing
comments on the verge of my origins

another moment where I grin
in the face of another meal
with too much or too little
another polite bowl of soup  strong
bread identified by salt or the hot
bite of peppers   another calendar
released at the border   another:
so long kiddo   welcome home sister—
girl, where've you been?

# With Josephine in Tangiers



*Cette a l'heure efficace c'est la bonne.*
This time they mean business.


at first it was all romance
the love of France and champagne

then the war and what she packs
is the baggage of memory

"they always come in the dead of night"
she says and watches the sky turn inside
out and curdle white

in the morning she trades bits of herself
for a spy's trick of black limo and night train

anything that can move swiftly  quietly
like some vague gesture leading her
west to Algeria or south to the Sahara

menagerie of leopard  monkey
and men dovetailed in her wake


*   *   *   *   *


she is surprised at how the dust
tracks of wars look familiar

she moves quickly  remembers
Harlem where prejudice lies
translucent under a patron's thumb

clothed in silk she is
a Fascist's dream perhaps or nightmare

but Moroccan land suits her skin
and she plies the Aryan fantasy of color
chocolate queen strolling in the sun

by June the yard will be cobbled with clay
still rutted from the pitch of a camel's steamer

and in the quicksand of scattered light
black shadows will weave a fabric of forms

she stretches   light moving
under liquid smile
neck, vertebrae, elbows, fingers

*   *   *   *   *

a spy knows the enemy depends on imagination
and white men expect "l'Afrique Primitif"
but she knows sensuality requires intelligence

and is ideal for the task
even nude each movement suggested
more than ever seen

her laughter unravelled in sand patterns
like oil textures inviting all eyes to follow

she drinks with the enemy
turns giddy from the garden's blossoms
her teeth gypsy silver hiding secrets

Josephine moving while light still blurs hues
of leaves and chance is all fragrance and shadow

Josephine: hiding behind fronds of bright colors
come show me what lies
between motion and rest

between violence and peace
and what I smell in the air from New York
to Tangiers and the ruins of Europe

Josephine, sweet Jo: heigh–di–ho
ma chérie, heigh–di–ho

# A Skardalija Walk in Three–Quarter Time

3 hats, 3 pigs, 2 fishermen and the stones
      in double rows of quaint cafes lined up 2 x 2
      for what could be any square in Greenwich or Soho
      the look the '50s the first time round
      count the wooden signs clanking like 100 tongues
count the taxis hungry for riders
      but do not count on the moon's light
      caught in this Balkan claptrap of stones
      or poets walking aimless and foreign
      in a country of endless walking and smoking
count only cafes called 3 pigs, 2 fishermen
a bad fiddler and a horn
      the wheels of thick farmer's bread
      the lambs skinned and hung like long-necked chickens
      hooked in place and round and round like humps of stone
take a stroll around square center, the usual statue of horse
      and rider, the museum cast in light of national treasures
      like that bust of a woman veiled in stone drawn and hard
      as her face beneath it, eyes turned inward and haunting
count heroes lounging in Slavic poses, cigarettes in place
      their women of little drinks and many sweets
      the paths cleared for lovers walking hand-in-glove
      their eyes on the moon flicking against stones
      like patterns in a gypsy's scarf
the usual dreck of moonlight and stones
fiddlers and sorrow, lovers and shadows
      now count gypsies begging for small change
      in a country that only holds little money
      their language so old it holds only vowels
count the words that echo against my tongue clean
      as the bad boots of that pigeon-toed poet
      walking beside me past guarded eyes
      where I may be African, American even
count the looks that pass between us
      the sweet cakes glazed in animal fat
      the goat's cheese, bouquets of radishes
      cevapcici and wine
count the hundreds of bridal gowns in a town
      where no wind blows harder than war
      and stones marry sorrow
ask my landlord who married the baker's daughter

ask the bread that sits on the table
        the tubs of spongy cheese
ask the women who stare at me and wonder
ask the men who stare and mutter
        the museum statue that sighs under her stone veil
        the gypsies married to stone
        my blackness wedded to their eyes

# Trompe L'oeil: Slovenia

This first glimpse of the eastern side of the Alps
and the driver turns his movie profile to the rear

view mirror dancing on the neap and ebb of springless
seats where I ride shoaling waves of cobblestones.

I am new at this—the chauffeured car, the driver
whose face I've only dreamed of outside GQ magazines.

He is taking me to the edge of tourists' maps
where, he grins, the sights are oldest and best.

We whisk by streets of handsome men in throaty shirts,
occasional statues of lock-jawed poets and patriots, all

men; this country is all about men—the driver's sly smile,
the sidewalk Lotharios, their women bent under strong bread

and onions, and children trying to live up to the legend,
staring as if it is their nature to be stupid.

I am just a break in their routine—my black face
despite the familiar car, a foreign blur racing by.

Inside hairpin curves, the driver's smile is slower;
with each casual roll of the wheel against his thumb

my heart turns in my mouth—he is taking me to see
the sights but what I see is another sad town strung out

in ever-thinning mountain air while the car,
German-made despite its lumpy seats, eats up the climb.

At the top I take his hand, half-grateful for its firm hold,
and the ground.  Before me the usual castle dungeon awaits.

Below, a postcard town.  I sigh, hurry in, hustled along by
another tourist wearing a zoom lens camera like a penis.

# Five Black Beauties Romancing Dalmatia

*with Angelita, Rosalind, Geneva, Anita ...*
*photographed in Dubrovnik one day in May*

*Keep dancing ... it's your only*
*ticket out of here.*

anyway, the place looks like a backlot for a bad Flynn movie
the standard castle, walled city, and that damned sea, always

the main character on this stage set where you stroll past
handsome Slavs grinning like extras waiting for a swordfight

you expect a dancer, some Gene Kelly or Michael Jackson
jitterbugging up the steps backwards like the rest of this mess

forever caught in the time warp of a bad film shoot
but what you get are waiters in long aprons and longer faces

and the sea rushing toward you like a fist
everything set to pounding rhythms of heavy rock bootlegged

off U.S. recordings, always misspelled—and all under the spell
of the sea wandering in hard with the same old ethnic problems

of tourists and armies and pirates—folks buying and selling
bodies (in this town the men, more beautiful, have better luck)

but as you walk past, pretty black, everybody stares, remembering
Turkish traders and the last time your kind appeared on this coast

finally, when we have grown sick of it all: the busses unloading
all those Germans and English and Swedes—or the sea performing

its one dance once too often—or one too many pimps (call them sea
birds) selling their bodies to any old woman travelling with money

we head for the hills where the slope of days, despite the hidden
promises, takes its own sweet time falling into the same old sea

everyone wonders how soon before our return
laughing, we keep them waiting

# Lifting the Morning

*for Sally and Salvatore*

On the Isle of Ischia we ate our morning
Meals just beyond a line of sleeping American
Bombs laid pillar to post beneath
The wine cellar's lime–washed walls.

The sun laughed among rocks painted
Dull metal–grey to match those souvenirs of war
Uninvited yet ingeniously placed in perfect fit,
And there, where I was more American than Black

Or almost Ethiopian, I came to know what else
Could fit Italian mornings: pastel houses shored
By a bedrock of bombs, the sea glinting
In the distance, and a mixture of languages

Circling the breakfast table like water seeking
Its own level.  I was fresh from months
Of struggling with uncertain Balkan light
And never questioned longing for that Neapolitan

Profusion of flower petals, bread, cheese
And the day's first rocksalt smell of the sea
Just before the water turns oily with sun.
In that garden of muted bombs, the sun blessed us

While behind us the mission church glowed white
With grief for sailors lost forever
In that perfect sea.  No storms touched us
Inside the garden's bleached light of morning,

And except for those sleeping bombs
And the radio's crackling disasters,
Only our laughter separated us
From houses crooked along narrow streets

In stark shades of magentas, pinks and blues,
So carefully toned I was reminded of crayoned
Clothes I once cut for paper dolls, my blunt-tipped
Scissors following twisted lines until I filled

Shoeboxes with outfits of bright colors snipped
In paper perfection.  I used those same crayons
To trace map lines where newsreels said Patton
Had taken his tanks and my father south

To the war in Africa.  I learned the names:
Napoli, Trapani, Pantelleria, Casablanca,
And beached my Janes and Bettes safely
Behind the lines where they poised in high–heels,

Pinups smiling at the lip of cardboard
Ridges as if waiting for suitors to request
The next dance or stroll around the shoebox deck.
In Ischia no suitors climbed streets

Cut in wavering steps between houses.
In that garden threaded with war memories
The sun quietly lapped at cotton candy
Colors trailing the quay's edge clear to Sicily.

If we took our coffee to the balcony and leaned
Against the chalky rail, we could imagine the sea
Pulled in a perfect blue line from the mission
Church to the African coast.  In that light, our arms

Touching the balustrades were definite hues
Echoing trails of wars we'd grown up to hate.
Sometimes we stayed there until the light changed,
And while the mission bell intoned the day's prayers

For lost sailors, and the sun baked houses
Into faded pastels as grey–blue as those bombs,
The sea would gather all light until colors bled
Like bright socks caught in a white wash.

# The Breakers at Split

*for Niki B.*

along the ocean wall, Germans
lie trundled in sleeping bags
their bodies zipped into black
canvas caskets like casualties
waiting for a seaside burial—
as we walk past, fresh
from a bed we have stunned with love,
a few turn to mutter useless
Teutonic oaths, but most
settle like the Adriatic
in waves of slumber

even then they lean
into some sort of awful precision
sleeping where the moon falls
across these Yugoslav waters in a single
line of determined light
like reflections from a door left ajar
at the end of some sleepstruck hallway—
by day, they walk hotel corridors
like real guests, devouring
tennis, surf, and the hostess bar

with rousing songs of last wars
words break like crystals
at the water's edge where
other Germans once turned the sea
red with bloodsweat—
but in this country the history
of bigotry lies
hard on everyone's face
and Germans are no more
than the next horde of tourists
sleeping with their bodies
always turned towards home

they have just eased
into the first crest of dreams
when we pass, our breaths
thick as sea air gone sodden
in the moon's unwavering light—
after we reach our rooms, I watch
the darkness grow even thicker
until all light dies and those sleeping
against the sea wall are no more
than black humps pocking blacker sand—
an hour later, the surprise of rain
seems sweeter beating
against their canvas sheets

# There's an Obi in the Dishwasher
## [and Other Useful Japanese Phrases]

*bullfights*   the old man who invites us in likes plums
        he knows we have come to buy his craft
        but he will not talk money
        that is for his wife
        he will play Kabuki melodies
        on his Steinway upright and count
        the plum pits we leave on our trays as thanks
        he shadow plays the fight
        long fingers copy the horns
        the table is the ring and his wood
        holds the mass and grace of the bulls
        two fight at once he shows
        we nod our heads in unison
        each move is important
        the way the bulls are pitted in the ring
        one man per bull to bow each animal's head
        until bull against bull brings the natural
        end to things  he explains

*Tsuyu*    to the sound of plum rain  he explains
(the rainy    how a strong bull seldom bellows
season)     but holds resolute for that moment
        of balance when one thrust counts
        each stroke of his knife copies the movements
        raw blocks of wood formed like the bull's bulk
        fine lines for hair and fiery eyes
        dyed chokeberry red
        we know all of this without words
        a sign and a smile for each idiom guides
        us through his workshop
        the smell of woodcurls and sap
        a little tea and the wife
        to barter and wrap what bit of this rainy
        night our carefully counted coins might buy

*mapping*   in Japan a house address is not counted
        by a slot on the street or measured
        steps from one door to the next
        one number is for the Shogunate
        another for the number of times the house

was rebuilt and still another for each owner
in St. Louis they have torn
down every house I ever lived in
the mental map I unfold in my sleep
bears no relation to the smudge of streets
that have dissolved neighborhoods of my relations
into unreadable addresses

***Yohaku***       now nothing is linear   nine does not follow
(space              ten and with half a brownstone gone
deliberately    best friends cannot live three doors down
left blank)       no numbers link me to the dark
                  centers of family and friends   the interior
                  black zone for "cullud" folks of cities
                  where streets meant safety are gone
                        vanished like each digit of the house
                        on Bellefountaine Grandma played
                        in her daily quest for a numbers win
                        or the walk-up on Kennerly
                        where the iceman was slain
                        the boyfriend's house at Creve Coeur (kids
                        said *Grieve Car* in Missouri French)
                        or the unholy stench of St. Ferdinand Avenue
                  not linked by the logic of numbers
                  just the disappearance of a dozen landmarks
                  where I learned to travel before I left home

***tourists***       because it is not enough to die at home
                  where accidents are as ordinary as salads
                  we are out here playing world travellers
                  with nothing between us and forever but English
                  each day of loving you requires a new map
                  full of convenient phrases where we spend
                  too much time putting subject before verb
                  still I'm amazed at how often I can lose you
                  the horizon of landmarks keeps changing
                  faster than our destination and language
                  fails us in countries we've yet to know
                  guidebooks offer no translations for that
                  we fear most   shouts like Kilroy's: Hello
                  I Was Here  You love Me   Stop the War

**Shinkansen**
(bullet train)

we still expect to be released by simple hellos
constructed on extra articles and prepositions
those English frills that keep us in taxis
but love is a language that suggests
more than we will ever say
ideographs of worlds that hold oceans
where concepts are altered by each line we make
we are mystified by words that allow
us to get lost every five minutes
regardless of our intentions
so we stay on the move   kissing air
waving goodbye in towns we thought we'd love
looking each year for another climate
to upset the balance of time and gravity
and all the laughter clicking with the awful
speed of a slick bullet train

# Part Two

*I learn by going where I have to go*

—Theodore Roethke

# Poetry Circuits

six times you've circled
the Original Overhead Door Company
and Buzzard Iron Works
the night guard is suspicious
and you are nowhere closer
to the nervous host who eagerly signed
you on this tour
here in the dark, you are lost
your hands clutching the panic
of steering wheel
and strange country lanes
somehow it is always picturesque
and somehow no service station
attendant has ever heard of the place

you remember the contract
the fistful of maps you received
in yesterday's mail
the arrows pointing to Twin Bears
Double Oaks, Middle Lake or Southshore
but hieroglyphics offer no solutions
to junctions of four–way signal lights
forked roads and train tracks
someone knew you were coming
this morning they removed all the street signs
everything is hidden
your audience  your patience
the big brick building they said you couldn't miss

you are on your way
contract signed   poems on the seat beside you
breathing their own fire
out there somewhere an audience waits
impatient as any lover
but the state map is fuzzy
and filled with community colleges
while you are convinced this town
has no schools or civic centers
you are lost in a forest of flat roofed
houses, back alleys and dirty factories

you imagine the laughter of the architect
who dreamed up the location in revenge
against his first grade teacher
you are convinced there are no maps
to cover this   it will always be raining
you will always be late
you will circle this town forever
your best poems glued to the seat beside
and withering with age

# Sojourn at the O'Neill Summer Theatre: 1987

this is the summer someone gave a mansion
we see it waiting—out there in sections
the balconied front half, the side wing, the back
so much like a scene shop, its bathroom side out
we wonder if there will be a play on Marat
but anything's possible in New England summers
where front lawns roll gently to Long Island Sound

mornings the actors warm–up in contralto
in tenor and bass and mile–high soprano
and interns look busy with messages posted
the grass is still dew swept, pianos tuned–up
this is the summer of music theatre
and sweet young composers in genius profile
throw delicate tantrums while house movers settle
on how much for moving half-chimneys one mile

writers are walking with ears to the ground
they try to remember the names of their characters
and oh how much easier to write without actors
and music and audience and critics and such
and directors demanding we move here and step there
and faster and slower and stop this right now
but the mansion stands patient, its wall paper heating
while the hot air of summer grows thicker by the hour

now the cook and the baker, the meal ticket taker
they've all done a bit of some stage work, they say
the snack bar is open, that kid is a comic
but everyone here is an actor of sorts, and lordy,
now I'm writing long-winded limericks
an old protest poet gnawing lyrical seeds
but that is the danger of being around theatre
you are who you never thought you were to be

by late afternoon there're new lines for the chorus
but we took out the chorus at ten minutes past noon
we'll read through the script because timing's important

but when no one was looking, the actors left the room
the music director decides to entertain us
he runs through a few bars of old Broadway scores
our visitor from China describes opera in Beijing
which doesn't seem half as undisciplined as ours

the evening's no different
we're drinking like actors
we're talking, we're moaning
the noise level's rising
the sailboats are gliding down Long Island Sound
we're eating like actors
in wolf bites of worry
roles are dismantled and scenes passed around
and finally we open and all seats are taken
the writers are pacing in back of the pews
I glance out the window, the mansion is silent
its windowless curtains are pinned back and smiling
it's waiting for next summer's theatre crew

# Free–Falling Nebraska

The mind's eye pins all we know to some horizon.
There we recall: shape, the absence of light or heat;
There we create: a place on the map, a spot to put our feet.

Then power blown–out and hot prairie sun suddenly eclipsed
Behind marble halls and stacks of books, and all I know
Is purged of light.  Despite archival tracts, I grope

For lines of spatial references, geometry that liquefies
In the rooted dark.  One missed step and I am lost,
Without fingerprints of landscapes and petulant weather.

Without sun or man–made light.  I am forced to close
My eyes but when I hold my breath, the darkness multiplies.
I am too tall to be the child told to swallow fear,

Who knows what moves out there has known the Brothers Grimm.
In sudden shadow I am weightless, calling out: *Who's
There?*  The answer echoed back: *Here.  And where*

*Are you?*  Where indeed?  I know what seems real is real
Only if in time it lives.  But this inconstant place leaves
Such little clues: flatness that surrounds completely,

The loss of sun—of stars—of heat,
Nothing held back or in between, including
Machines to thin out prairie air too thick

For breath or gears designed to make clear water run
Uphill in a place where there are no hills.  On this
Prairie everyone leans into the imagination of valleys

And weather, so one hand extended, I creep
Toward that distant voice, try to hold the world inside
Awakening motor noises, knowing so much of what is

Artificial keeps life tolerable in a country
That can flatten out and vanish in the next whirlwind.

# What the Jackrabbits Know

How wives swallow dry prairie grass
Eating like songs its madness  how swollen
Rivers fill with sickly children  how
Earth becomes the sole language of men

Indians remember naming this country for
Nettle rash and flat water  now

Lakes still cook in fresco heat and
In humid dreams county–long trains moan
Night long like lonely bison listen:
Country music wallows in the sweat
Of old time horsey smells and
Lost tent preachers  until
No one dies without the sound

# Jerry and Newt and That's All Folks!

*We have art so that we*
*may not die of reality.*
　　　　　　　—Nietzsche

the ballet will tour out of town this year
they left without funding and we grew ill
in the sudden absence of fierce beauty

to dance one day is to live a week in luxury
but there was nothing to welcome us to this season
where the movement of sand and stars no longer feeds us

suddenly feet and hands grow smooth as dinner plates
and buildings once tolerated for their solitary history
perish in the artless dust of bankruptcy

a town that fails to discover the poetry of dance dies
of its own momentum  autumn smells of words turn rancid
tabby cats take on Siamese faces and refuse to be stroked

rooms wilt with bits of rabbit fur torn from toe shoes
and tiaras slip into holes between walls and mirrors
while bodies become parodies of themselves

Dr. Suess is gone and a thin layer of reality settles in
and the rabbits run lickety-split while the town
sleeps circled by hawks and doves

# Wild Parrots Have Taken to Wintering in Ballard

I ride the hump of street
rising like a wave above the tunnel
its underground roar permeates
traffic  I was content with a dead

city beneath the city  the secret alleys
the coffee cups spiderwebbed and waiting
but this grid is warmed with diesel fumes
and out here among crows and gulls I become

no more than a flash of blue feathers
squawking someone else's words:
*love*money*save*new*easy*free*

the guy digging up the street
tries showing me the underworld
but there are things I don't want
to know  he moves sheets of metal

like the earth's tectonic plates
his fork distanced from its source
the grid open and looming

he grins  beckons me toward it
fat and white he stands his ground
regards me like some trick of light

something brought up from the sluice
where bricks smell like chalk
soaked in piss and rats

walk on stilts
lurching like savannah beasts
wounded by tourists

Cousteau's ghost is around the corner
waiting for the right turn of brick
against skull to mark
my evolution

*honor* I say: *sing a song * sing a song*
it's language however you slice it
I wait for the others to join me
they come in slowly

we're dying out here and we
know it  that odor sweet
as arsenic fills the holes

# Heavy in the S–Curves

dusk and someone's dog runs
loose on the freeway

Xs and Os blink randomly
at the end of no turn lanes

a child speaks of piety and faith
reborn in arenas where ghosts
of lions prowl restless edges

your ticket is invalid
the traffic so close you lick rubber

two ducks mistake a drain puddle
for the lake at the end of the block
yachts doze in the lapping waves

the decadence of a child's mother
glows like incandescent light
under velvet shades

breathless the dog runs
his nails shatter and bleed

insects frenzy in gathering darkness
feed on the last of day's light

the news echoes inside static
the music loud enough
to keg–tap your heart

transparent spiders drum impatient
tunes: dust  dust  and more dust

it ends so fast
a knife in a vacant lot  a crackhouse:
a landscape of studied resentments

road grids threaten your wheels
studs mark which lane goes
you ride the bumps to stay awake

a cricket's click  a chest rale
a moving van shifts gears on upgrades
searches air gentrified

what you see in the dog's eyes:
we have all learned to be victims

the Xs change to neon
the Os drift in silence
geese quarrel in the approaching dark

# The End of Civilization as We Know It

*In Florida, hundreds of monkeys now living along the Silver River
are descendants of eight monkeys brought here from Africa and
abandoned after the 1930s Tarzan films.*

along the river where fish with redpetal gills
swim endless circles, monkeys still tell stories
of a time when the camera's whir and Tarzan's
yell filled the space where the sun shifts
below the tree line from neon white to green

they feed off the whisper and hum of trip switches
the chirr where that baldface call, so wordless,
so close to an order other than their own
waits in wave pulses of voice and wire
behind electric eyes holding Tarzan's cry

the river has divided them into warring clans:
those on the southern shore claiming
shimmering thickets where turtles nose down sand
banks in rotten scuttles of water, and on the other
side the northern clan hurling insults across lines

of whistling reeds and sweet paths of blackthorn—
at night they taunt each other like street gangs
with chittering talk of who was king and who servant
but of the old country they remember nothing except
the vague smell of the sea drifting into the ship's hold

without Tarzan they have lost the claim
to their moment in lights—now war is the order
of the day and the smell of fur is heavy as gunpowder—
they have only what we have left them with:
a private line to the time when cameras blurred

day and night in a necromancy of all things wild—
Tarzan's cry no longer holds the currency of our fantasy
with Africa—and the parents of parents who believed
relax fat and happy behind suburban walls
debating what is to be done about the monkey wars

just listen: some nights they trip the electric eyes
until dawn just for the hell of calling him up: Tarzan
in the orison of 78 rpm—Tarzan and everything
is bared: teeth for a fight or penis erect to mate—
always it is Tarzan: his loin cloth slung

like a butcher's apron—Tarzan: with bananas and lollies
and how the world would be all right as long as he was
landlord—Tarzan: you old sound bite lost among alligators
and birds murmuring in the lugubrious shadows of gum trees—
Tarzan! Tarzan! Why hast thou forsaken us?

# Delsey in the Window

every morning except sunday
delsey owns only the world she sees

    behind thick glass
    she questions in silent
    meows all that falls between
    windowledge to elm or pine

alley to crosswalk
but sundays delsey takes a long

    catstretch on the top step
    then stalks the faint scent

of dogs and crossing guards
galoshes and idiot mittens
she takes stoic note of weeklong

    homework in large block letters
    starchy school lunches and impatient
    parents waiting for patient teachers
    watches all my movements past her house

delsey needs no tenure to rule
her kingdom and marks the currency
of my pitiful labors

    in eyesful of green laughter
    she trusts few of her kind
    and none of any other
    but on sundays the world is truly

delsey's and free of catteasing
children, my ghetto superstitions
all folks about the business

    of making business work regardless
    of weather or who will tip the cabbie
    rake the lawn or find junior's knit cap
    it's sunday and delsey no longer

keeps the window as shield
its cold breath her only companion

      she bathes in the casual light
      of sunday until her sleek black
      body is nubian pretty
      her catprints on the roof

of my car are proof of her presence
clover petals of dust where wiperblades
have left half–crescent deserts

      these mark her leisurely passage
      when on sundays delsey crosses
      my path without asking

# Chitin

Winter flies are fat and dulled
By the warmth of artificial heat
They seem as surprised to be here
Still as we are to see them
Hiding in the room's smallest corners
They drone with the self–pity of loneliness
Begging for eternal sleep
Winter flies are pallbearers from some forgotten
Funeral where relatives have thoughtlessly
Walled them in the mausoleum
They are drunks awakening in bars
Long after closing hours when all the bawdy
Girls have gone home, laughing
Awakened, they vaguely remember light filtered
Through a thousand holes of wire mesh screens
Like tiny pinpoints of eyes, the bottle
Green air of summer, the sour nectar
Of decay or sudden wash of a swatter
But it is winter and they fumble
With death in feeble circles, rubbing their legs
Together in dispirited fashion like desperate
Heroes signalling from abandoned hills
Of window ledges where their papery bodies
Curl into that moment of final submission
And rooms are filled with one last shriek
Of nasty interruption, a desolate whine
Replete with promises they cannot keep
Poor filthy little buggers

# Junkyards and Gangways

city dogs strutting like gangsters
    in frayed leather jackets
    like seedy money lenders with shifty
        eyes sniffing out competition
        marking boundaries the old way
            with noondrizzles of urine
city dogs checking pantcuffs
    and which alleys are good for nibs
    knifekeen dogs with pedestrian airs
        zigzagging and challenging cars
        stopping at crosswalks with the right
            light and pulsebeat of traffic
city dogs all sleek in clipped suburbs
    where poodles own their masters
    and tiny dogs rule with needleteeth
        or blockbound nobreed ruffians
        whose bodies broadcast their beginnings
            the head of one mongrel the tail
            of another and coats speckled
            like some old man's skin
city dogs taking on any bigot's sins
    cold noses cataloguing colors easy
    as a racist for suspect or friend
        knowing one hand bites clean as another
city bitches with teats like shopping bags
    or bowbreeched studs commanding random
    packs set to a noseful of some errand
        machinegun growls goading stray children
city dogs of no real origins
    vicious by nature or nasty in old age
    full of silent knowledge and eyes
        that carry lost names like Lout or Whippett
        and the memory of skulking and whining
city dogs with long lazy tongues lapping
    up the dawn and allnight barking
    in homemade codes of offrhythm signals
        steamy coats worn thin at the haunch
        like a widow's fur
            and clammy in thick city air

# Why the Sea is for Salty Dogs

the walrus bleary–eyed waits
at the edge of the cliff
his mission he says
is to watch the ocean
for signs of rogue waves
but I have come along
at just the moment when his occupation
has grown stale
and is no longer self–serving
so he latches onto my coat tails

his own leaving long wet furrows
and the litter of years in the sand
he is my shadow  a great bladder I drag
unwillingly along
a raucous noise behind whiskers
white with age looking just a little
like Lenin on a bad day
stomach dragging the ground and that fat
ass slapping against the last tide
going out

on our first date we just talked
gulls feathered the sky trying to imitate
swans and doves while sea water
splashed into coffee cups and behind him
a banner burning with the cachet: I am the eggman!
his constant talk lulled even neap tides

now I can't believe I found any comfort
in his bearish body
or that I fell for the same old story
of being mislead by sententious kings
and waxy seas—the noise I mistook
for a song of rebellion

he showed me whales sounding and turtle
shells imprinted with battle scars
face it, I was impressed

even when he fell asleep between one
stride and the next
the folds of his skin smelling
of the spice of distant oceans
roasted chestnuts  a pipeful of apple
cured tobacco  and those eyes a trick
of sea green kelp and star fish

# Shelley at Sequim Inlet

Gull you never were a bird to float
on balmy breeze   high on a manure pile
you were king   your feet planted firm
as a farmer's boots   the smell suits
your dirty white coat   bird that is gull
you are no romantic speck hovering
in search of scraps   warm rot or rust
dirty bird you bully this northwest coast
and any other that offers loot   heavy-winged
you circle spews of foam as if some great
gossip nailed you to the spot   hawking
for gang wars   keeping the neighborhood
awake just to break your brother's back
      What gall you have gull
      What open lust and luck
      What single eye and hip–broke walk
no petal soft bearing whips you toward garbage
fighting's your only relief from the constant
call for food   and heaven is the air
alive with the smell of dead things
come on gull   voodoo caller of the sea   riffraff
faker   we know you   despite your shrill delight
your cracked–beak squawks say you're grey with fear

# To the Crow Perched on
# Chief Sealth's Fingertips

Poised on the Chief's outstretched
Arm, you chastise the world:
One eye turned groundward,
The other tilted up toward
The first sign of sky emptying
Itself of light into that bright
Something held in your beak.
       Omen–bird of darkness, you've picked
       The right altar for your sermon:
       A dead Indian's extended arm,
       The safety of this square where
       Men who pass statues like this, no sooner
       Believe its warning than your shrill calls—

CRAZ–CRAZ! (*Tomorrow Tomorrow!*"—what a word
—*Tomorrow!*: time in doubt for us all!)

Old Queen of Shades, Faith–weaver, why
This puny statue for your stage
When it was you who left your 3–toed footprints
Near the eyes of the Goddess Crone,
       And rooked many another wise woman?
       And why does, Raven, harbinger of doom,
       Pretend to jump to Jim Crow tunes—spindly-
       Legged Rastus hiding knowledge behind a face
       So thin, bones seem trapped on the outside.
       And you calling to the sun: "*Tomorrow*
       *Tomorrow!*" the cry half–stuck in your throat
       While your sister, Magpie, forever oracular
       Boasts her lies and summons a crowd squawking:

*"One bird for sorrow. Two for luck. No more
tomorrow."* Chattering Maggie, Magog, Mayper—

Old girl, were you among the thousand blackbirds
Released in a dance of wings swinging
Low over Florence Mills' Harlem grave?
A murder of crows followed her woes
As clearly as maize follows rain.
I watch you now, old Witch's Foot, work
A soft shoe Disney would envy as you dance

Bare-knuckled across someone else's dream.
Even Disney knew dancing is what you do best.
> He was there when you fled Ewondo
> With buttons and bleached cotton string
> In payment for a ghetto full of stolen
> Brer Rabbits and Aunt Nancys,
> Words you invented each night
> By rearranging sixty-four sizes and shapes
> Of leaves to follow your Trickster lust.

And now, one more lousy trick of dark and light,
And me—of course without a camera.

So Bird, why waste your three-claw
Jig in this urban village
Mall where no man will take serious
Note of your summons and no one
Here can record how the silhouette
Of your foot clipped to the sun
Symbolizes Peace or Death? (*What a joke—*
*All these lives with no questions of self.*)
> Why here and not some foreign shore,
> Like Mauritania where, your cousin, Kraken,
> Claims she owns the ridge-pole spines
> Of grey elephants?  One is slaughtered every
> Ten minutes as she marks day's end,
> Bloodied ivory nagging light into pleats
> Of the open sea.  And the beach stained

Copper with the fading cries of dead souls
No two-footed, sloe-footed bird can hold.

But here you are balanced, first one foot
Then another in perfect symmetry of prestidigitus
Attitude—a bird feathered in primigenial night,
Old NEVERMORE himself, pirouetting on Sealth's
Final warning to keep tomorrow away from the grey haze
And bruised afternoon sun flecked with Seattle's
Awful history, where all that is breathtaking
Is breath taking.

You there, in your cackle of oily black feathers
Preening in a series of flashy jétès,
Why wink as if I will surely believe
Chief Sealth's statue hangs from your claws,
And you hang from the sky and own this square
And all that you see—beginning with the colors
Baked in my scarf and me, groping for words

To paint you standing in a pose that this day
Or another, you think I'd never dare quote.

# Part Three

*Peculiar travel suggestions are*
*dancing lessons from God.*

—Kurt Vonnegut

# Man Dances to Death in Storm



> *In the spring of 1980, during one of*
> *Seattle's freak thunderstorms, a young*
> *man climbed to the roof of a building*
> *where he danced in the nude until the*
> *winds blew him off to his death.*
>
> *In Seattle, rain drives everyone*
> *to the brink of death.*
> —The Stranger
>
> *If I could prove what I know, do you*
> *think I'd be here now?*
> —Joan Crawford in Rain

With all our knowledge, we are still victims of weather,
dancing to the madness of sun or rain
when all we need know is that the body is the sum
total of all that is unknown, and each dancer
hoping to rob the stars of their predictability,
has no sense of knowing when it all began—
the frenzy of constant weather, like sunstroke
leaving the skin craggy and aching to be shed.
> It is not easy to answer the call of water,
> to listen to the drone of it beckoning us
> like the beat of loosened tongues
> unrolling curses held in the tight
> oath of centuries.

How can we know what goes on while we are dreaming?
In this weather even fish get clamped fin and tail rot
and the soul, dangerously clinging to the body's image,
must follow the natural order of weather, its power
held in check, resting silent and electric
in the corners of rooms where heat has bathed us
in the sweat of imagined lovers.
> Even now this room is a moving jungle
> of atoms battering each other
> like starving birds, while our bodies
> shed skin, hair, nails
> and this poem turns bad with random anger.

Know now that each breath is a chain of events,
that madness is no more than the pull of the moon.
Look, someone has been drawing lines in the sky
and below that a flat roof smudged
with the flumes of fog and rain—
the horizon barely inked in and holding
a luminous figure, his limbs drawing
circles like wires in motion.
                   While winds whistle a murderous chant,
                   an ozone of blue light claims
                   his skeleton in four, five, six seconds
                   of death before the storm slams
                   into itself.

How many of us long to follow him in that final fall
for good from too many days of unnamed obsessions,
to know what he has known when the horizon won't hold
us to one fixed point and, tightly bound to atoms,
the flesh rolls back to sinew and marrow,
the arms whip out in one last human gesture?

Given half the chance, we know what we do to ourselves,
what melds the dancer to the dance until the body
unfurls and we ride lovely in our bones.
                   How much of this madness has to do with weather
                   or how we forget what marks the track
                   of the beast—how as we fall free
                   of our bodies, the wind mocks our silent howls
                   and the rain drums with laughter?

# Drawing in the Dark—
# A Jazz Monochrome



*for Miles Davis 1925–1991*


**1. tenor sax**

Each landscape has its own remark for our lives

      nothing is as you imagined
        sidemen, slidemen
      tomorrow's moonlight
        your children


anything moving howls through the night like scavengers
    rooting for a place in line where foxes stroll
      and snipes slip quietly to shore

      old now, your face holds
    to the beauty of its own repose
your skin turned blacker than black from drugs
      while the memory of melody laughs quietly

**2. bass**

what we learn from
    a body that fails to feed us
    makes us all want to write a book
    we turn instead to what we think we hear
where

the inside of the world is the underbelly
of light and magic we enter knowing
instinctively so much of what we are
is conceived in the dark
        in the cup of mysterious sizes
            a slag of earth healed over itself
                the sea trapped in a conch shell


**3. trumpet**

colors are the lies we tell to keep death at bay
        when night brings sounds so close they take
        for themselves a form that knows only color

then old men rise from bar stools and run
        their ash black hands through
            beard stubbles knowing the feeling

arouses
        memories in the knees of old women too
            accustomed to kitchen floors, eyesight gone
                shadows pulled around them comfortable
                    as half forgotten songs

# Fascinating Rhythm

got this picture of my mother sitting
behind a coat with a fox collar up
to her chin and Stella by Starlight
hairdo—smoke already in her eyes

listen: saucy sassy Sarah cutting
each song like a silhouette
on a rainy street turned bluesy
inside a lone saxophone

night sky knuckled against the horizon
daylight still a thin blade of light

folks saying: you got to catch that act
down at Club Riviera got a glass bar
and a chandelier like the star system
Orion—and me sitting up in there

got on my high heels
and don't care attitude and folks
saying: child's legs so skinny
they look like burnt spaghetti

the club didn't let out before dawn
sneaking home to catch the sunrise

next day all them church folks
saying: too scary too low down
too loud but ohh honey that voice
just pure God lovely

Billie?
Honey when I was young
I said nobody wanted
to hear that cracked
voice and besides:

she ain't *even* pretty
then went out and found myself
some Gardenia cologne

Ella: scatting on a high note
make the birds sit up and sing

Lena Horne and Georgia Brown
sweet and full of satisfaction
that first glass of champagne
to taste—to savor like stormy
weather from a garden supreme

girlfriend could turn that voice
inside out and smooth as kid leather

# Eads Bridge Boogie Across
the Mississippi

The way Mama tells it I didn't have the good sense
God gave a chinch much less know to stay away from fast
tail gals who danced across that river into evil Illinois.
But I was sixteen—you know the age—dreaming
about draping myself across some smoky piano, stocking
seams bone straight and skirt hiked thigh high
like Tina Turner on those nights when she was still
strutting low down in kitchen table clubs.  I was jail
bait—a gun moll in my dreams—flying high inside
husky voice blues beside some boy with a come-on look till
the sun came up and I went racing racing home before
that dishwater light caught me on the wrong side
of the Mississippi—the bridge railings slicing shadows
across the water whuckity-whuck like Chuck Berry's guitar.
And that sweet brown boy with the gimme-some eyes
trying to turn sober and both of us, like Mama said:
looking like hell sued for murder.

# While Her Knees Keep A–Knockin and Her Toes Keep A–Rockin

*for Chakema*

when vivian picked me up
in her Detroit mo–bile
we were riding high
      understand—high
      was the operative word
      brandies mixed
      like our blood lines
(so potent they almost
exploded by their lonesome)
and we always used our secret
names (hers was Cherokee—
mine Mandarin) styling with flash
      in high high heels
      hanging our legs
      out the window  long curves
      ending in stilettos
dangerous as daggers
we awakened the longing
of many a–passing man
we were Kansas City
Windy City  Any City
      get it  we were fast
      gaining our practice
      chasing babies busses
      bad boys  or running
to board some airplane
on three inch spikes
even that weekend we stopped
on the Oregon coast
      tried to make a fire
      without breaking
      our lacquered nails
we took the stuff
bad girls were made of
      fashioned it to suit
      until Monday morning

when we reported
crisp as aprons for work
and white folks asked  all polite
and distant  how we'd spent
            our weekend  just hanging
            out we said  just hanging

# A Charleston for Florence Mills

1895–1927

      Josephine
      might have been
the toast of Paris, but Florence
just shimmied out of that blasè slouch
held by Broadway queens from cabarets
on Dover St. right on down to Dixie
        Sissle and Blake
        Put and Take
hoi polloi running wild with only six years
of limelight and Florence girl dancing knock–
knees and flying legs as if nickel
subways would end that day—and they did
        Bye Bye Blackbird
        sing high 'n strut
unlike sister, Hardfoot Maude, just Florence
stepping feather light, crooning:  *I'm just*
*a little Blackbird waiting for a Bluebird too*
and satin garters popped for the hardluck '20s
        oh buckdance
        and cakewalk
and kicks that mimicked slaves, Florence out
dancing for the Prince of Wales, 20 times some
said in that certain age when darktown shuffle
was de rigueur for matrons of the dark tower
        comedy streaks
        jocose tricks
yes, all the vogue was jazz for Baby Florence
with her circles and shakes and feet skipping
like polished stones while ribbons of arms
danced with a flame too brightly held but some
        said Panama
        took the cake
to see Florence dance the shimmy shake
with a smile so wide it hurts still

# Way Out Wardell Plays Belgrade

we are looking for a cafe
and this Serbian dude
who knows more than I
he thinks of why
blacks play the blues
      swears the place is hot
      all I know is
      I'm forced to walk the nine blocks
      from my flat no cars
      here just uneven Belgrade streets
      and the air old
as intrigue
held by his memory of a steady thump
thump splat ohh jazz beat
and a drummer trying to play
it loose and easy and all   around
the next bend he says
at every turn
      but we won't turn back
      even though bricks are slick
      with rain soaked soot
      and cabbies cheat
      for any amount in native tongue
      and by the time my knees begin
      to ache we've reached
a stretch of bistros
marked by smoke in a city
where even pigeons
peck at butts
in the rudeness of gutters
as if waiting for someone
to toss them a light
but here     nothing is thrown away
      except laughter
      and we enter after listening
      to a woman drunk on wishing
      laughing to hug a man
      too poor to buy another beer
      and too stubborn to kiss her
and when we step through the door
my black face brings all talk
to a halt until the only sound

left in the shuffle
of feet is the bass
and some rhubarb player
trying to imitate a Harlem scat
            in broken Slavic
            and all of them waiting silent
            for my approval while he
            chokes on the sadness of every note

# You Dance and I Laugh for the Joy
# of Dancing to Nothing

*After seeing "A Study in Nothing"—*
*a ballet by Pearl Primus, who was known*
*as Omowale: 'child returned home'*


Tanka:
    First islands then home
    sun–danced Dunham's Latin beats
    African palette
    half–circles given to air
    spin dreams savage butterfly

    Etude:
        weaving stories like Zora Neale, first islands then home
        your ballets no apologies for Hard Times Blues or lonely
        sun–danced Dunham's Latin beats   those who were upset
        melted as you danced an African palette
        of music torn from the caves of our black hearts
        half–circles given to air and shouting rhythms where part
        of what we are is lost   no day better than when you dance
        Pearl   when you get the beauty of it hot, we cry
        and beg you to spin dreams savage, butterfly


Tanka:
    feet arched like cupped hands
    dance shadowing Africa
    ebony lightning
    whirlpool turns inside heartbeats
    leaps graze a singular sky

    Etude:
        Primus articulate   feet arched like cupped hands
        your fluid Ceremonials more than Broadway boogie   can–can
        dance shadowing Africa too easily
        for Cafe Society patrons   balletomania thinking their measly
        history could dull your skin   ebony lightning
        flash of reach beyond wind   frightening
        whirlpool turns inside heartbeats
        where dance is life  a balm against anger's heat
        you know it, baby   child beckoned home to fly
        where leaps graze a singular sky

# Sprung Sonnet for Dorothy Dandridge

*1923–1965*

A woman unadorned stands out in a crowd of otherwise
Camouflaged women, and takes from her shelf all manner
Of potions and powers, the oils and slick pots of colors
That hold electricity and confusion of mimicry
That test the ties that bind deception to reality
A woman in sundappled skin can mislead with mad
Confusion and tricks that others would give an eyetooth for
These are the women who step away from themselves
Who know elaboration gives us our most handsome species
Who teach us disguised animals need not dissolve
Into surroundings when anonymity is not our destiny
Who know to understand the zebra's stripes, you must get down
   On your hands and knees where the vertical whites vanish
   Into the sky and the blacks take on a shape so indistinct
   The world's a blurred kaleidoscope of the mundane and bizarre

Where Whites say white with black/Blacks say black with white

# Bo Jangles Visits the Studio

*To his own people, Robinson
became a modern John Henry
who instead of driving steel,
laid down iron taps.*
                    —Jazz Dance


hip hop ain't no hula hoop
backs of legs out front
        electric boogie
        knock–kneed bird of the Zulu nation
                chicken pecking

hip hopping out of devastated lots
out of Crenshaw Heights and Watts

shadow dancing out of devastated lots
masamba minswele mbele

hip grinding break beat
                raptitude
                attitude
        uprock  side step

this leaf never falls
tack head dancers
        steel band drummers
        move and freeze

jingle–jangle quarrel and wrangle
every step a pearl

carried double pistols  step back
tap tough as any bird

pop a wave to the hand
through shoulders and down
        pass the current  aim
                raptitude
                aptitude
        keep the song low
        solo lights  music  now  video

# Square Dancing the Adriatic

no matter how you cut
it you can't get
there                                      from
                                           here          grab a train   a bus
                                                          a plane  grab a boat
                                                          anything that moves
                                           grab
a hint  of Black
descendants in a town
called Ulcinj—hidden
naturally in back of
this ragged backwater
country full of Turks
and other unseemingly     dark
                                           folks         take that road,  left
                                                          the right fork,  turn
                                                          lady,  you  are
                                           for
                                           sure
                                           lost!
listen to Dubrovnik
rug merchants [that's
the trick and                              those
                                           dudes
                                           have          all the clues]  never
                                                          mind if they speak
                                                          without breaking a
                                                          flirt, honey

                                           this
                                           story
earns a history of
dinners back on home
turf                                       :hire
                                           a car         —some dashing Slav
                                                          on his first time out
                                                          who will drive break
                                                          neck roads at night
                                                          with no headlights—
                                                          forget those ditches
                                                          filled with rotting
                                                          hulks of
                                           tour
                                           busses

stay off the bus stay
off the boat don't
walk   the end is
near—get it? –no
sweat:   danger is          your
                            middle
                            name            now enter  Medjugorje
                                            town of ugly pilgrims
                                            watching pretty
                                            virgins high on wheat
                                            germ and boredom
                                            pray for the real
                                            Mary to star in their
                                            tv road show
                            babe you
                            best get
                            out
while you have
someplace to go—draw
a line from your head
to the nearest border       —ask            the gypsy on the
                                            corner—she knows a
                                            Greek driver who has
                                            been here before
                            you can
                            awaken
in Albania groaning
through Act Six of a
five hour King Lear
by gypsies—Kabuki
style—it never ends        get it?         so ignore  that sweet
                                            British critic beside
                                            you  he is a maniac
                                            for bleak landscapes
                                            and may keep you here
                            forever
unless you head for
the coast the path a
sheer drop from
cliffside to ocean
down to Adriatic surf       :follow         goats to the hut: 3rd
                                            from center with some

guy who's a caramel
replica of your 2nd
cousin's husband

[can't
you
remember?

—the cat who came
home from Chicago
with no teeth and
eight fingers!] but
now this *dragi's*
talking to you—
and he's

like
suspicious        so use language you
can muster—better
make the accent
Jamaican in case he
hates

Americans

and don't slobber
he's kin,  just a few
too many generations
removed—so don't
sweat it 'cause  with        next
year's
war        he'll hardly have
time to remember your
name—just give the
high sign—say:
*Cheese*

say:

*Hi,        moj        Covjeck!*
say: *Yeah,*

*Soul*        *Brother!*

# Paris Subway Tango

*for Edna Daigre*


> *somebody almost walked off*
> *with all of my stuff*
> —Ntozake Shange


at best you can say
your judgment was tainted
by movies and old
expectations
      Paris equals passion
      n'est pas?      so why not ride
         the subway just this one
         night despite
         all the echoes of caution
         dancin : in your head
         and how even in Harlem
         you have a thousand
reasons to stay above
ground instead
of ruttin : beneath
the fabric of some city
that seems clipped
from a Romare Bearden
nightmare book
      but this is Paris
      Chagall and Degas
and men whose eyes fill
with mysteries
of North African deserts
         so the first brush
         of body against body
and you get this wild rush
of good sense fightin : desire
yellin : I *want* ** *I don't want*
like salt messin : with perfume
         and although his face
         flirts with your imagination
         his hand's dippin : into your purse
         so, baby, you fling aside all caution

lay him out with a one–two step
swingin : hip to hip
like when you used to
Arthur–Murray–in–a–hurry
    part Hustle : part Hucklebuck
    matchin : his every tightass turn
    groovin : between track and train
                        like the two of you been
                        practicin : M*T*V
except your purse is the cash prize
so do it, girl, cause
maybe this home–boy–Arab
don't know you
ain't takin : no shit
even if you gotta tango
on this metro clear to the end

# Hooking Up with Ray Charles and the Great Percy Sledge in Madagascar

Seven o'clock in downtown Tana and I pry
my eyes open for one more day
of bread and too sweet tea while the bugler
rouses soldiers from the army barracks
at the foot of the hill
and city morning radio plays

yet another cut of Ray Charles wailing
*I got a woman... yeah, yeah.*
Taking the hint the concierge
practices English cutting in
for the last three words *ohh yeah...*
while on the terrace of the hillside

villa above my veranda a woman watches
as her husband pounds rice,
the sound bouncing from my commode
to the wrought iron gate until
the whole hill shakes with each thrust.
In the valley below even the city

shimmering in morning mist seems
to tremble against that pestle,
the buildings blurred like fingers
waving to the thickening morning sky.
I know it is nearly eight when
the wood cutter begins his climb
up one hundred fifty steps to the next street.
He stops to check out my breakfast table

as Ray Charles moans *way cross town... ohh yeah*
and the hillside pulses against the rice pestle.
The concierge brings in fresh baguettes
of long french bread brown as the limbs
of the poinsettia tree (yes, I'm still surprised
to see they're not sold in little green pots
behind some hardware store).  Their branches
stretched and gangly as the legs of the boy

who buys and sells bottles and follows
the woodsman up the steep incline while
morning radio lets Ray slide into Percy Sledge
and everyone stops to listen to his guidelines
of what makes loving last. (Here he's practically
a national hero.)  The concierge cuts in slick
as a Sunday dancer gathering all the right words
as Percy's last chorus collapses

into *when a man love love loves a woman...*
He leaves me dreaming of my lover
thousands of miles from this veranda
where that damn bugler makes sure everyone's
awake and I trade bad French for more tea,
and read my usual breakfast
of baguette, stairstep streets
and ohh yeah, sweet morning radio.

# Puerto Cristo

*The caves on Majorca were hiding places*
*for the Moors invading the Spanish coast*
*until the Spaniards poured hot tar*
*into the caves' opening.*

Some say
Angels sleep
In the Caves of Ham
Their crystalized wings
Touch floor to ceiling
Some say
Their laughter
Is the sound we hear
Through the pipe organ
On board the barge
That seven days a week
Traces for tourists
Stalactites that almost
Kiss the glassy surface
Of a lake so clear
And deep and cold
Only blind fish live there
And the boatman merely
Goes along for the ride

# Poem for Kitaro Written at
# a Nude Beach on the Adriatic

*for Larry Levis  1946-1996*

*A woman who disowns herself can
sit on any beach*
                Character Sketch of a Woman
                Looking,  Elva Pèrez–Treviño


Yugoslavs say the sea
is so great no one sees
its end

tides are signs
of things to come and what
the wind tells us


at home the bridge
tender's horn is toned
down for day barges

the sounds at night
penetrate
all four walls

in these waters
any touch is the kiss
of fish swimming past

fingertips  fish
*ptese   ptesca*
so close in each language


we are what the sea wants
what the wind allows
when dreams

give geography
to what we dare think while awake
we look back and see what works

how one line suggests
more than we knew
in dreams or water

strange things happen where
no one looks at flesh where
earth takes its star shape

Sweet Jesus we are here
naked under the moon's pull
where the voice of the ocean

is the only memory
that allows surprise

# Sunrise: 40,000 Feet

at this altitude time
jerks us out of season
crossing the date line
sometimes takes years
only the sky remains
the same turning blue
from stone grey to clouds
as hopeful as pillows
given the chance we
could share this
if not weeks
then days
where we've wandered like Bedouins
in a bad spell of weather
we've come to believe
we're here where godly time
reaches the human psyche
nothing ever touching us but
air so pure

# Caution: This Woman Brakes
# for Memories

When the air is thin with frost
I blow rings of ice smoke
as I did when I was young
and imagined myself grown
and never answering to anyone.
From smoke rings to pots
that became helmets and tanks,
I play-acted a world where
color held no name and eyes
were tears holding light.

Without knowing the contours
of earth, any rock
can become mountain, and puddles
vast oceans of many-legged beasts.
None of this is new.
All children are urged
to wander through the screen
of what is real before
they are pushed into the serious
matter of living where they lose

the surprise of believing.
We become adults with only a toehold
on fantasy, like ghost light from a torn retina
vanishing in the corner of the eye where, half
blind, we learn when to turn a phrase or bend
a letter until *o* becomes *e* or *3*
evolves into *8* and less simple digits.
No easy idiot graffiti of *girl*
into *gril*, but *loan*
into *god* and *home* into *bog*.
One blink and a sign that reads:
*Warning: Truck Makes Wide Turns*
can be misread as *Caution: This*
*Woman Breaks for Every Turn*
and everything is possible.

Yesterday as I crossed the flag
stones of a posh hotel foyer
I saw a fat rat grey and sleek
claws clicking like loose chains
on the slick tiles when he moved.
I heard him yell: *look at me go in and out*
*of revolving doors, go pitty pat*
*on my rat-like feet, go into fake*
*sunshine and champagne and home.*

The silk calla lilies nodded yes
and I believed them.

Today on the beach at La Push, logs became
chairs, dead bears, boats with roots like stars and
I was a ship sailing back to the beginning.